AWS VPC

(Virtual Private Cloud)

Beginner's Guide

George Sammons

Copyright©2016 by George Sammons

Table of Contents

Disclaimer

While all attempts have been made to verify the information provided in this book, the author does assume any responsibility for errors, omissions, or contrary interpretations of the subject matter contained within. The information provided in this book is for educational and entertainment purposes only. The reader is responsible for his or her own actions and the author does not accept any responsibilities for any liabilities or damages, real or perceived, resulting from the use of this information.

The trademarks that are used are without any consent, and the publication of the trademark is without permission or backing by the trademark owner. All trademarks and brands within this book are for clarifying purposes only and are the owned by the owners themselves, not affiliated with this document.

Introduction

The need for the use of Amazon Web Services (AWS) is on the rise. This calls for the need for us to learn how to launch the resources of the AWS into virtual networks, and we have to define such networks. The Amazon VPC is an effective way of helping us do this. This book explores this in detail. Enjoy reading!

Chapter 1- What is Amazon VPC?

The Amazon VPC (Virtual Private Cloud) allows us to launch the resources of Amazon Web Services (AWS) into a virtual network which we have defined. The virtual network is similar to the traditional network which one would have operated in their own data center, with the advantages associated with the use of the AWS scalable infrastructure.

The Basic Concepts of Amazon VPC

Before starting to work with the AWS VPC, it is good for you to understand some of its basic concepts, and know the difference or similarity between it and your network. Let us discuss these concepts:

1. VPCs and Subnets

   A VPC is a network whose dedication is on your account. It has been logically separated logically from the rest of the networks in AWS Cloud. One is capable of launching their AWS resources such as the Amazon EC2 instances into their VPC. You can also perform a configuration on your VPC, add the correct IP address, configure route tables, and create subnets, network gateways, and security settings.

A subnet is used to represent the set of valid IP addresses in your VPC. The AWS resources can be launched into the subnet which you have selected. If the resources have to be connected to the Internet, then you have to use a public subnet, and use a private subnet if there is no need for the resources to be connected to the Internet.

If you need to protect the AWS resources which are contained in the subnet, then it will be good for you to use multiple security layers, such as network access control lists and security groups.

2. Supported platforms

After Amazon EC2 was released for the first time, it could only support a single flat network which was shared with the rest of the customers, and the platform was known as "EC2-Classic." AWS accounts which are old enough are still in support of this platform, and they are in a position to launch instances into either a VPC or EC2-Classic.

Once you have launched your instances into the VPC rather than the EC2-Classic, you will be in a position to:

Give static private IP addresses to the instances which persist between the starts and the stops.

Run the instances on single-tenant hardware.

Give multiple IP addresses to the instances.

Change the membership of the security group for the instances once they are running.

Define the network interfaces, and then attach one or more of the network interfaces to the instances.

Add an addition access control layer to the instances in the form of Access Control Lists (ACLs).

Default and Nondefault VPCs

In case your account supports only the EC2-VPC platform, it has to come with a default VPC which has a default subnet in each of the Availability Zones. A default VPC will offer the advantages of a EC2-VPC, and it is always ready to be used. In case you have a default VPC and then you fail to perform a specification of the subnet when launching an instance, the instance will be launched into the default VPC. Instances can be launched into the default VPC without the need to know anything regarding the Amazon VPC.

Regardless of the VPC which your account can support, it is possible for you to create your own VPC, and then perform the configuration in the way that you need. This is referred to as the "nondefault VPC." The subnets which are created in the non-default VPC and the ones which are created in the default VPC are usually known as the "nondefault subnets."

Accessing the Internet

You are in a position to control how the instances which you launch into the VPC access the resources which are outside the VPC. Your default VPC will include the Internet gateway, and each of the default subnet will be a public subnet. Each of the instances which has been launched into the default subnet will have a private IP address and then a public IP address. The instances are in a position to communicate with each other via the Internet gateway. The purpose of an Internet gateway is to permit your instances to establish a connection to the Internet via the network edge of Amazon EC2.

The Internet access for an instance can be enabled even though the instance might have been launched from a non-default subnet. For this to be done, the Internet gateway has to be attached to its VPC and then associate the instance with an elastic IP address.

Alternatively, if you need to allow an instance in the VPC to establish an outbound connection into the Internet but prevent any unsolicited inbound connections from your Internet, you can take advantage of a NAT (Network Address translation) device. A NAT device can be used for the purpose of mapping multiple private IP addresses to a public IP address, and a single one. A NAT device should have an elastic IP address and an Internet gateway is used for connecting it to the Internet. An instance in a private subnet can be connected to the Internet via a NAT device, which will route traffic from the instance to the Internet gateway, and any responses will be routed to the instance.

Access to a Home or Corporate Network

One can choose to connect their VPC to a corporate data center which they own, and this is done by use of an IPsec hardware VPN connection, and the AWS Cloud will be made an extension of the data center.

A VPN connection is made up of a virtual private gateway attached to the VPC, plus a customer gateway which can be found in the data center. The VPN concentrator in this case is the Virtual Private Gateway, and this can be found on the Amazon side of our VPN connection. The customer gateway has to be a physical device or a software appliance which is located on your side in the VPN connection.

Chapter 2- VPC Security

Amazon has implemented three features to ensure that their VPC has been secured. These include the following:

Security groups- this works like a firewall for the associated Amazon EC2 instances, and it is responsible for controlling both the inbound and outbound traffic at the instance level.

Flow logs- these are responsible for capturing information about IP traffic which is going to and from the network interfaces in the VPC.

Network Access Control Lists (NACLs)- these work like the firewalls for the associated subnets, and they control both the inbound and the outbound traffic at the subnet level.

After launching an instance in the VPC, it is possible for you to associate it with any of the security groups which you have created. It is possible for each instance in the VPC to belong to a different set of the security groups. Sometimes, you may fail to specify the security group for your instance when you are launching the instance, and then it will turn out that the instance will use the default security group for your VPC.

You can use any security groups for the purpose of securing your VPC instances. However, one can choose to add the network ACLs as the second security mechanism. After creating a flow log for the VPC, it will be possible for you to monitor any rejected IP traffic moving in and out of the VPC. A network interface card can be used for this purpose. The flow log data will have to be published to the CloudWatch Logs, and this is good for the purpose of diagnosing the permissive network ACL and security group rules.

You can make use of Access Management and AWS Identity for the purpose of controlling who in the organization can be in a position to create and manage security groups, flow logs, and network ACLs. You can choose to give this permission only to network administrators but not to the personnel who will need to launch the instances.

The Amazon network ACLs and security groups will not filter traffic to or from the AWS-reserved addresses or link-local addresses. The reserved addresses are the first four and the last one in each of the subnets. Similarly, the flow logs will not capture the IP traffic to or from the reserved IP addresses. These reserved IP addresses are used for the provision of services such as Domain Host Configuration Protocol (DHCP), Domain Name Server (DNS), Key Management Service (KMS), and the Amazon EC2 Instance. It is also possible for you to configure an additional firewall in the instances which will help you in blocking of network communications with the link-local addresses.

Security Groups in VPC

A security group works like a virtual firewall for the instance for the purpose of controlling inbound and outbound traffic. After the launching of an instance in a VPC, one can choose to assign the instance to over five security groups. Security groups will work at the instance level, but not at the subnet level. This means that each instance in the subnet of our VPC can be assigned to another set of the security groups. If you don't specify a particular group when launching the instance, the default security group in this instance will be assigned to the instance.

For each of our security groups, one has to create some security rules which will be responsible for controlling the inbound traffic to our instances, and you will also have to define a separate set of rules which will control the outbound traffic. You may choose to setup your network ACLs by using the rules of the security groups so that you may be in a position to add an additional security layer to your VPC.

Basics of Security Groups

Security groups in VPCs are characterized by the following:

Allow rules can be specified, but not deny rules.

Separate rules can be specified for both the inbound and the outbound traffic.

One is allowed to create up to 500 security groups for each VPC. Up to 50 rules can be created for each of the security groups, and up to five security groups can be associated with each network interface.

The default setting is that no inbound traffic is allowed until you have added the inbound rules to the security group.

Network interfaces and security groups are associated. Once you have launched an instance, it will be possible for you to change the security group which is associated with an interface, and this will also change the security groups which are associated with our primary network interface. It is also possible for you to change the security groups which are associated with any of our network interfaces.

The instances which are associated with a particular security group are not able to talk to each other unless you have chosen to add some rules which will allow for this.

The default setting is that the outbound rules will allow all of the outbound traffic. This rule can be removed and then outbound rules added which will only allow some specific outbound traffic. However, this is only when you need it to operate like so.

The security groups are always stateful. Response to the allowed inbound traffic will be allowed to flow outbound, despite the outbound rules, and the vice versa is true.

The VPC you are using must have come with a default security GROUP; Each EC2 instance which has been launched inside the VPC will have to be associated with a default security group, if you fail to specify a security group during the time of launching the instance. The default security group is associated with its own rules, and it is good for you to know more about these rules. However, the good thing is that these default rules for the default security group can be changed, but it will be good for you to be sure of what you are doing.

Security Group Rules

The rules for a particular security group can be added or removed. This is usually referred to as authorizing or revoking. A rule must apply to either inbound traffic OR OUTBOUND traffic. Access can be granted to a specific CIDR range, OR MAYBE to another security group in the VPC OR IN a peer VPC.

A security group rule is made up of the following parts:

The traffic source (Security group or CIDR range) and the port range or destination port. This applies only to the inbound rules.

The traffic destination (a security group or a CIDR range) and the destination port range or the port. This applies only to the outbound traffic.

Any protocol having a protocol number. In case you have specified ICMP as the protocol, it will be possible for you to specify any or all of the ICMP codes and types.

In case your instance at host A initiates some traffic to host B and makes use of the protocol other than UDP, TCP, or ICMP, the instance of the firewall will track only the protocol number and IP addresses so as to allow response traffic from host B.
In case host B initiates the traffic to the instance in a separate request within a period of 600 seconds of your original request or response, the instance will accept it regardless of the security rules for the group rules for the inbound security group.

The reason behind this is because it has to be regarded as the response traffic. This can be controlled by modifying the outbound rules for your security group, and this will enable you to permit only a number of outbound traffic. Also, the network ACL for the subnet can be used. The reason for this is that the network ACLs are stateless, and the automatic setting is that they don't allow response traffic.

Once a security group has been specified as the source for our rule, the instances associated with the source security group will be allowed to access the instances which are located in the security group. Note that with this, no security rules will be added from the source security group to the current security group.

Some systems which can be used for setting up the firewalls are in a position to allow you to perform filtering on the source ports. Security groups allow people to filter only at the destination ports.

After the addition or removal of rules, all the instances associated with the security group have to be updated about it. The type of instance will determine the kind of rules that you add. Consider the examples given below for the security groups for the web servers. The servers have the capability to send either HTTP or HTTPs traffic, and then send MYSQL or SQL traffic to our database.

0.0.0.0/0- this is for the TCP protocol on port 80. It is used for allowing inbound access by HTTP from anywhere. The port 443 for this is used for allowing the inbound access by HTTPs from anywhere.

1. Public IP address range for your network- This is for the TCP protocol on the ports 22 and 3389. The port 22 is used for allowing the inbound access by SSH in Linux instances from the network. This is usually over our Internet gateway.

2. Security ID for database servers- this is for the TCP protocol on ports 1433 and 3306.The port 1433 is used

for allowing Ms SQL server to access the instances in the security group that you specify. The port 3306 is used for allowing a MySQL server to access the instances in the security group that you specify.

In the case of a database, it will have to access a different set of the rules.

Stale Security Group Rules

If the VPC has a VPC peering connection to another VPC, a rule for the security group security can be used for the purpose of referencing another security group in our peer VPC. With this, the instances which are associated with the security group which has been referenced to establish communications with the instances will be associated with the security group which they are referencing.

If the person who owns the peer VPC which is operating deletes the security group which has been referenced, or in case the owner or you delete the connection of the peer VPC, the security group will have to be marked as stale. The rules for a stale security group can be deleted just as you would have done to delete a normal security group rule.

Modification of a Default Security Group

The VPC comes with a default security group which will prevent all of your inbound traffic, but allow all of the outbound traffic and allow all the traffic between the instances in the group. The group can be deleted, and it is also possible for you to change the rules for the group.

Creation of a Security Group

We have said that the VPC comes with a default security group, and you can use it. However, you may need to create your own security group so that you can be able to reflect the different roles that the instances are playing in your system. The following steps are necessary for you to create a security group:

1. Open the console for Amazon VPC.

2. Choose "Security Groups" from the navigation pane.

3. Choose the option "Create Security Group."

4. Provide a name for the security group, and then add a description to it. From the VPC menu, identify your VPC ID and then select it. You can then choose Yes, Create.

You will then be done, very quickly and simply. By default, once you have created a new security instance, it will have only an outbound rule which will allow all the traffic to leave the instances. For you to make any other changes, then you have to create some rules.

Addition and Removal of Rules

After addition or removal of a rule, it is good for you to remember that any instance attached to the security group has to be updated about the same. However, with the Amazon EC2 or the command line, it will be impossible for you to change the rules. However, you are allowed to add or delete rules. With the Amazon VPC console, it is possible for you to modify the already existing rules.

To add a rule, follow the steps given below:

1. Begin by launching the Amazon VPC console.

2. Choose *"Security Groups"* from the navigation pane.

3. Choose the security group which you need to update. The pane for *"details"* will display the details regarding the security group, plus the tabs for working with the inbound rules for the security group, as well as the inbound rules.

4. Communication can also be allowed between all the instances which are associated with the security group. On the tab for "Inbound Rules," select "All Traffic" from the "Type" list. You can then begin to type in the ID of the security group for the "Source," and you will be provided with a list of security groups. From this group, select your security group and then click on "Save."

5. If you wish, feel free to use the tab for "Outbound Rules" to add the rules for the outbound traffic.

Deletion of a Rule

1. Begin by launching the Amazon VPC console.

2. Select "Security Group" from the navigation tab.

3. Choose the security group which you need to update. The pane for *"details"* will display the details regarding the security group, plus the tabs for working with the inbound rules for the security group, as well as the inbound rules.

4. Click on "Edit," choose the role which you need to update, and then select "Remove, Save."

A security group with the instance in the VPC assigned can be changed once the instance has been launched. After making the change, the instance can be running or stopped.

To change the instance for a security group, follow the steps given below:

1. Begin by launching the Amazon EC2 console.

2. Choose "Instances" from the navigation pane.

3. Right click, launch the context menu for your instance, and then select "Networking, Change Security Groups."

4. In the dialog box for "Change Security Groups," choose either one or more security groups and then select the option "Assign Security Gro

Deletion of a Security Group

A security group can only be deleted if no instances associated with it exist. These instances include both the ones stopped and the ones running. The instances can be assigned to another security group before deletion of the security group can be done. The default security group can also be deleted.

To delete a group, follow the steps given below:

1. Begin by launching the Amazon VPC console.
2. Select "Security Groups" from the navigation pane.

3. Select the security group which you need to delete, and then select "Security Group Actions, Delete Security Group."

4. In the dialog box for "Delete Security Group," select "Yes, Delete."

Network ACLs

An ACL (network access control list) is an optional security layer for the VPC which acts as a firewall for the purpose of controlling traffic in and out of the subnets. Network ACLs can be set up with rules which are like the security groups so as to add an additional security layer to your VPC.

The following basics should be noted regarding the Network ACLs:

The VPC usually comes with a default Network ACL which can be modified. The default setting for this is that it will allow all the inbound and outbound traffic.

A network ACL can be associated with multiple subnets, but the vice versa is not true, as a subnet can only associated with a single ACL. After associating a network ACL with a particular subnet, then the previous association has to be removed.

A custom network ACL can be created and then associated with a particular subnet. The default setting is that a custom network ACL will deny all inbound and outbound traffic until you have added the necessary rules.

A network ACL is made up of a numbered list of network rules and these have to be evaluated in an order, beginning with the one with the least number, and this will help determine whether the traffic will be allowed in or out of the subnet which is associated with the network ACL. The number 32766 is the highest value which can be used for numbering a network rule.

The network ACLs are stateless, the responses to the allowed inbound traffic are subject to the rules for the outbound traffic, and the vice versa is true.

Each network ALC has got some separate inbound and outbound rules, and each rule can be used to either allow or deny traffic.

 Each subnet contained in your VPC has to be associated to a network ACL. However, some people will not do this. In such a case, the default network ACL will be used for this subnet.

Rules for Network ACL

Rules can be added or removed from the default network ACL, or create some additional network ACLs for the VPC. After addition or removal of the rules for a network ACL, the changes will be applied to the subnets which are associated with it.

A network ACL is made up of the following rules:

The Rule Number- evaluation of the rules is done beginning with lowest numbered rule. Once a rule has matched traffic, it has to be evaluated regardless of the presence of any higher-valued number which may be contradicting it.

Protocol- any protocol can be specified provided it has a specified protocol number. In case ICMP is specified as the protocol, you will be in a position to specify some or all of the ICMP codes and types.

Traffic source and the destination port or port range. Note that this applies to the inbound rules only.

The traffic destination and the destination port or port range. However, this will only apply to the outbound rules.

A choice of either ALLOWS or DENY for our traffic.

Default Network ACL

The default network ACL for the VPC has already been configured so that it can allow in all the traffic and allow it out, provided it regards the subnet which it has been associated with. Each of the network ACLs has a rule in which an asterisk has been used as the rule number. The rule will ensure that if a packet does not match any of our numbered rules, it will be denied access. The rule can be modified or removed.

Determining the Associations for a Network ACL

The Amazon VPC console can be used for the purpose of identifying the network ACL which is associated with a particular subnet. It is possible for a network ACL to be associated with more than one subnet, meaning that you are in a position to determine the subnets which are associated with your network ACL.

If you need to determine the network ACL which is associated with your subnet, follow the steps given below:

Begin by launching Amazon VPC console.

Choose "Subnets" from the navigation pane, and then choose the subnet which you need.

The network ACL which is associated with your subnet is part of the tab "Network ACL" together with the rules for the network ACLs.

To determine the network ACL which is associated with your subnet, follow the steps given below:

Begin by launching the Amazon VPC console.

Choose "Network ACLs" from the navigation pane. The column for "Associated With" is used for indicating the associated subnets for each of our network ACLs.

Select the network ACL.

In the pane for details, select "Subnet Associations" so as to display the subnets which are associated with the network ACL.

Creation of a Network ACL

It is possible for you to create a custom network ACL for your VPC. The default setting is that after creating a network ACL, it will be blocking all the inbound and outbound traffic until you have added rules. You also have to note that the ACL will not be associated to any subnet until you have associated it with one.

These steps can be followed for you to create a network ACL:

Begin by launching the Amazon VPC console.

Choose "Network ACLs" from the navigation pane.

Click on "Create Network ACL."

In the dialog box which appears, give a name to your ACL, and then choose an ID for the VPC from the list of the VPCs. You can then click on "Create, Save."

Addition and Deletion of Rules

After an addition or a deletion of an ACL rule, the subnets which are associated with the rule will have to be updated about the same. There is no need for you to terminate or relaunch the instances which are in your subnet since the changes will only be effected after a short while.

For those using the command line or the Amazon EC2 API, it will be impossible for you to modify the rules. You are only allowed to add or delete rules. However, individuals using the Amaxon VPC console are allowed to modify the entries for any rules.

The console will work by removing the current rule and then adding another one for you. If there is a need for you to change the order of the rule for the ACL, a new rule has to be added with the rule number for the new rule, and the original rule has to be deleted.

If you are in need of changing the order of the rules contained in the ACL, a new rule has to be added together with the number for the new rule, and then the original rule deleted.

The following steps can be followed for adding the rules for a network ACL:

Begin by launching the Amazon VPC console.

Select "Network ACLs" from the navigation pane.

From the details pane, select either the "Inbound Rules" or the "Outbound Rules" tab, and this will be determined by the kind of rule which need to be added. Once done, click on "Edit."

In the option for "Rule #," enter the number for the rule. Note that the network rule number that you add should not have been used in the network ACL. The rules have to be processed in an order, and this is done from the rule with the smallest number. It will be good for you to leave some gaps between the rule numbers. With this, it will be easy for you to add a new rule, and you will not be expected to renumber any existing rule.

From the Type list, select a rule. An example is when you need to add a rule for HTTPs. In this case, you will have to select "HTTPs." If you need to add a rule which will help in allowing in TCP traffic, select "All TCP." It is good for you to note that in some cases, the port number will be filled in for you, so you don't have to be worried about that. If you need to use a particular protocol but it has not been listed, you can select the option for "Custom Protocol Rule."

In case you need to create a custom protocol rule, you can select the protocol number and the name from the "Protocol" list.

In case the protocol which you have selected is in need of a rule number, enter the number of the port, or the port range, and use a hyphen to separate.

In the field for "Source" or "Destination" (this will be determined based on whether you are creating an inbound or an outbound rule), provide the CIDR range which the rule applies to.

From the list for "Allow/Deny," choose "ALLOW" so as to allow the specified traffic, or choose "DENY" so as to deny the specified traffic.

If you need to add another rule, select "Add another Rule" and then go through steps 4 and 9.

After completing, click on "Save."

If you need to delete a rule from the network ACL, follow the steps given below:
Begin by launching the Amazon VPC console.

Select "Network ACLs" from the navigation pane and then choose your network ACL.

From the pane for details, select the option for "Inbound Rules" or "Outbound Rules" and then click on Edit. Identify the rule which you need to delete, and then choose the "Remove" option for it. Once done, click on "Save".

If you need to associate the rules of the network ACL with the specific subnet, then the subnet has to be associated to the network ACL. A network ACL can be associated with multiple subnets, but a subnet can only be associated with a single network ACL. If there exists a subnet which is yet to be associated with a network ACL, then the system will automatically associate it with the default network ACL.

The process of associating a subnet with a default network ACL can be done as follows:

Begin by launching the Amazon EC2 console.

Choose "Network ACLs" from the navigation pane, and then choose the necessary network ACL.

In the pane for details, on the tab for "Subnet Associations," select "Edit." Select the box for "Associate," and this should be for the subnet which you need to associate with your network ACL. You can then click on "Save."

It is also possible for you to dissociate a subnet from a network ACL. If you do that, then the subnet will have to be associated with the default network ACL automatically. This can be done by following the steps given below:

Begin by launching the Amazon VPC console.

Select "Network ACLs" from the navigation pane, and then choose the network ACL.

In the pane for details, select the tab for "Network Association s".

Click on "Edit" and then click on the box for the subnet so as to deselect it. Click on "Save."

The network ACL for a particular subnet can also be changed. Note that after creating a subnet for the first time, it is automatically associated to the default network ACL. However, you may need to change this and associate the subnet to a custom network ACL. You should know that after you have changed this, there will be no need for you to terminate the instances which are running and then relaunch them, as the changes will be effected automatically.

The network ACL association for a subnet can be changed as follows:

Begin by launching the Amazon VPC console.

Choose "Subnets" from the navigation pane, and then choose the subnet you need to change.

Select the tab for "Network ACL," and then click on "Edit."

Choose the network ACL which you need to associate your subnet with from the list of "Network ACL," and then select "Save."

Deletion of a Network ACL

A network ACL can be deleted if and only if it has no subnets which are associated with it. It is impossible for you to delete the default network ACL.
The following steps can be followed to delete a network ACL:

Begin by launching the Amazon VPC console.

Select "Network ACLs" from the navigation pane.

Choose the network ACL which is to be deleted, and then click on "Delete."

A confirmation dialog will appear. Click on "Yes, Delete."

Chapter 3- Controlling Access to the Resources

Managing a VPC

Consider the policy given below which can be used for management of a VPC.

- {

"Version": "2016-04-17",

"Statement":[{

"Effect":"Allow",

"Action":["ec2:*Vpc*",

    "ec2:*Subnet*",

    "ec2:*Gateway*",

    "ec2:*Vpn*",

    "ec2:*Route*",

    "ec2:*Address*",

    "ec2:*SecurityGroup*",

    "ec2:*NetworkAcl*",

    "ec2:*DhcpOptions*",

    "ec2:RunInstances",

    "ec2:StopInstances",

    "ec2:StartInstances",

```json
        "ec2:TerminateInstances",
        "ec2:Describe*"],
    "Resource":"*"
    }
   ]
  }
```

In the policy, wildcards have been used for the purpose of specifying all the actions for each of our objects. Alternatively, you can choose to list all the actions explicitly.

The "Resource" as an element has used wildcards for the purpose of indicating that the user can specify the resources by use of the API actions.

The Amazon VPC also supports the Read-only policy. Consider the policy given below for granting users permission so as to list their VPC components. They will not be able to create, delete, or update them. Here is the policy:

```json
{
    "Version": "2016-04-17",
    "Statement":[{
    "Effect":"Allow",
    "Action":["ec2:DescribeVpcs",
        "ec2:DescribeSubnets",
```

```json
          "ec2:DescribeInternetGateways",
          "ec2:DescribeCustomerGateways",
          "ec2:DescribeVpnGateways",
          "ec2:DescribeVpnConnections",
          "ec2:DescribeRouteTables",
          "ec2:DescribeAddresses",
          "ec2:DescribeSecurityGroups",
          "ec2:DescribeNetworkAcls",
          "ec2:DescribeDhcpOptions",
          "ec2:DescribeTags",
          "ec2:DescribeInstances"],
      "Resource":"*"
    }
  ]
}
```

Amazon VPC Custom Policy

Consider the policy given below which will grant users permission to be able to launch instances, stop the instances, terminate instances, start instances, and then describe the resources which are available for the Amazon EC2 and the Amazon VPC. Here is the policy:

```
{
  "Version": "2016-04-17",
  "Statement":[{
    "Effect":"Allow",
    "Action":["ec2:RunInstances",
        "ec2:StopInstances",
        "ec2:StartInstances",
        "ec2:TerminateInstances",
        "ec2:Describe*"],
    "Resource":"*"
  },
  {
    "Effect":"Deny",
    "NotAction":["ec2:RunInstances",
        "ec2:StopInstances",
        "ec2:StartInstances",
        "ec2:TerminateInstances",
        "ec2:Describe*"],
```

```
    "Resource":"*"
   }
  ]
}
```

The second statement in the above policy has been used for the purpose of protecting the policy against any other policy which may grant the user access to the wider range of API actions by explicitly denying the permissions.

Instances can also be launched into a specific subnet. Consider the policy given below, which has been used for granting permission to be able to launch instances into some specific subnet, and then make use of a specific security group in the policy. Here is the policy:

```
{
  "Version": "2016-04-17",
  "Statement": [{
    "Effect": "Allow",
    "Action": "ec2:RunInstances",
    "Resource": [
      "arn:aws:ec2:REGION::image/ami-*",
      "arn:aws:ec2:REGION:ACCOUNT:instance/*",
      "arn:aws:ec2:REGION:ACCOUNT:subnet/subnet-14f5cg3",
```

```
          "arn:aws:ec2:REGION:ACCOUNT:network-
interface/*",

        "arn:aws:ec2:REGION:ACCOUNT:volume/*",

        "arn:aws:ec2:REGION:ACCOUNT:key-pair/*",


        "arn:aws:ec2:REGION:ACCOUNT:security-
group/sg-14f5cg3t3"

    ]
  }
  ]
}
```

We can also choose to launch instances into a specific VPC. Consider the policy given below, which can be used for granting a user permission to be able to launch instances into any of the subnets within some specified VPC. This is done by application of a condition key to our subnet resource. Here is the policy:

```
{
  "Version": "2016-04-17",
  "Statement": [{
    "Effect": "Allow",
    "Action": "ec2:RunInstances",
    "Resource":
"arn:aws:ec2:REGION:ACCOUNT:subnet/*",
```

```json
      "Condition": {
        "StringEquals": {
          "ec2:Vpc":
"arn:aws:ec2:REGION:ACCOUNT:vpc/vpc-14f5cg3"
        }
      }
    },
    {
      "Effect": "Allow",
      "Action": "ec2:RunInstances",
      "Resource": "arn:aws:ec2:REGION::image/ami-*",
      "Condition": {
        "StringEquals": {
          "ec2:ResourceTag/department": "dev"
        }
      }
    },
    {
      "Effect": "Allow",
      "Action": "ec2:RunInstances",
      "Resource": [
        "arn:aws:ec2:REGION:ACCOUNT:instance/*",
        "arn:aws:ec2:REGION:ACCOUNT:volume/*",

        "arn:aws:ec2:REGION:ACCOUNT:network-interface/*",
```

```
      "arn:aws:ec2:REGION:ACCOUNT:key-pair/*",

      "arn:aws:ec2:REGION:ACCOUNT:security-
group/*"
    ]
  }
 ]
}
```

Management of VPC Security Groups

The policy given below will work by granting a user permission to perform a creation and deletion of inbound and outbound traffic rules for any of the security groups within a specified VPC. This will be done by application of a condition key to the resource of the security group for "Authorize" and "Revoke" actions.

The second statement is responsible for granting the user permission to describe the available security groups. This is of great importance so that the users can be in a position to modify the rules of the security group by use of the CLI. Here is the policy:

```json
{
"Version": "2016-04-17",
  "Statement":[{
    "Effect":"Allow",
    "Action": [
      "ec2:AuthorizeSecurityGroupIngress",
      "ec2:AuthorizeSecurityGroupEgress",
      "ec2:RevokeSecurityGroupIngress",
      "ec2:RevokeSecurityGroupEgress"],
    "Resource":
"arn:aws:ec2:REGION:ACCOUNT:security-group/*",

    "Condition": {
     "StringEquals": {
       "ec2:Vpc":
"arn:aws:ec2:REGION:ACCOUNT:vpc/vpc-14f5cg3"
     }
    }
   },
   {
    "Effect": "Allow",
    "Action": "ec2:DescribeSecurityGroups",
    "Resource": "*"
   }
  ]
}
```

Creation and Managing of VPC Peering Connections

The policies given below can be used for the purpose of creation and modification of the VPC peering connections.

Creation of a VPC Peering Connection

The policy given below can be used for the purpose of creation of VPC peering connection requests by use of the VPCs which are only tagged with "Purpose=Peering." The first statement will apply a condition key.

The second statement will grant the user permission to create a VPC peering connection resource, and this make it able to use the wildcard character instead of the resource ID. Here is the policy:

```
{
"Version": "2016-04-17",
"Statement":[{
 "Effect":"Allow",
```

```json
"Action": "ec2:CreateVpcPeeringConnection",
"Resource":
"arn:aws:ec2:REGION:ACCOUNT:vpc/*",
 "Condition": {
  "StringEquals": {
   "ec2:ResourceTag/Purpose": "Peering"
  }
 }
},
{
"Effect": "Allow",
 "Action": "ec2:CreateVpcPeeringConnection",

 "Resource":    "arn:aws:ec2:REGION:ACCOUNT:vpc-peering-connection/*"
}
]
}
```

Consider the policy given below, which will allow users for a specific AWS account to be able to create VPC peering connections by use of the VPC in region "us-east-1." Here is the policy:

```json
{
"Version": "2016-04-17",
```

```json
"Statement": [{
 "Effect":"Allow",
 "Action": "ec2:CreateVpcPeeringConnection",

 "Resource": "arn:aws:ec2:us-east-1:333333333333:vpc/*"
},
{
 "Effect": "Allow",
 "Action": "ec2:CreateVpcPeeringConnection",
 "Resource": "arn:aws:ec2:REGION:333333333333:vpc-peering-connection/*",

 "Condition": {
  "ArnEquals": {

   "ec2:AccepterVpc": "arn:aws:ec2:REGION:777788889999:vpc/vpc-aaa111bb"
  }
 }
}
]
}
```

Acceptance of a VPC Peering Connection

Consider the policy given below, which will allow the users to accept the VPC peering connections only from a specified AWS account. With this, users will be protected against acceptance of connections from accounts which are unknown. The first statement in this has used a condition key for the purpose of enforcing this. Here is the policy:

```
{
"Version": "2016-04-17",
"Statement":[{
 "Effect":"Allow",
 "Action": "ec2:AcceptVpcPeeringConnection",

 "Resource":    "arn:aws:ec2:REGION:ACCOUNT:vpc-peering-connection/*",

  "Condition": {
   "ArnEquals": {
    "ec2:RequesterVpc":
"arn:aws:ec2:REGION:444455556666:vpc/*"
   }
  }
 },
```

```json
      {
    "Effect": "Allow",
    "Action": "ec2:AcceptVpcPeeringConnection",

     "Resource":
"arn:aws:ec2:REGION:ACCOUNT:vpc/*",

    "Condition": {
    "StringEquals": {
     "ec2:ResourceTag/Purpose": "Peering"
      }
      }
      }
    ]
    }
```

Deletion of a VPC Peering Connection

The policy given below will allow users of a particular account to delete the connections of VPC peering except the ones from a specified account which still exists in the same VPC. Here is the policy:

```
{
"Version": "2016-04-17",
"Statement": [{
  "Effect":"Allow",
  "Action": "ec2:DeleteVpcPeeringConnection",

  "Resource":
"arn:aws:ec2:REGION:444455556666:vpc-peering-connection/*",

  "Condition": {
   "ArnNotEquals": {
    "ec2:AccepterVpc":
"arn:aws:ec2:REGION:444455556666:vpc/vpc-14f5cg3",

    "ec2:RequesterVpc":
"arn:aws:ec2:REGION:444455556666:vpc/vpc-14f5cg3"

   }
```

```
    }
  }
 ]
}
```

Working within an Account

The policy given below will allow a user to work with the VPC peering connections wholly in a specified account. Here is the policy:

```
{
"Version": "2016-04-17",
"Statement": [{
 "Effect": "Allow",
 "Action": "ec2:DescribeVpcPeeringConnections",
 "Resource": "*"
 },
 {
  "Effect": "Allow",

  "Action":
["ec2:CreateVpcPeeringConnection","ec2:AcceptVpc
PeeringConnection"],

  "Resource": "arn:aws:ec2:*:333333333333:vpc/*"
 },
```

```json
    {
      "Effect": "Allow",
      "Action": "ec2:*VpcPeeringConnection",

      "Resource":        "arn:aws:ec2:*:333333333333:vpc-
peering-connection/*",

      "Condition": {
       "ArnEquals": {

         "ec2:AccepterVpc":
"arn:aws:ec2:*:333333333333:vpc/*",

         "ec2:RequesterVpc":
"arn:aws:ec2:*:333333333333:vpc/*"

        }
       }
      }
    ]
  }
```

Creation and Management of VPC endpoints

The policy given below will give the users permission for creation, modifying, viewing, and deletion of the VPC endpoints:

```
{
  "Version": "2016-04-17",
  "Statement":[{
  "Effect":"Allow",
  "Action":"ec2:*VpcEndpoint*",
  "Resource":"*"
   }
 ]
}
```

Some policies will allow the users to work only with some specific parts of the VPC console. Let us discuss these.

Use of the VPC Wizard

The VPC wizard can be used in the VPC console for creating, setting up, and configuring a VPC. The wizard will provide you with a number of configurations which can suit your requirements.

A VPC having a Single Subnet

The first configuration for the VPC wizard will create a VPC having a single subnet. The policy should be as follows:

```
{
  "Version": "2016-04-17",
  "Statement": [{
    "Effect": "Allow",
    "Action": [

      "ec2:CreateVpc",                    "ec2:CreateSubnet",
  "ec2:DescribeAvailabilityZones",
  "ec2:DescribeVpcEndpointServices",

      "ec2:CreateRouteTable",          "ec2:CreateRoute",
  "ec2:CreateInternetGateway",
```

```json
    "ec2:AttachInternetGateway",
"ec2:AssociateRouteTable",
"ec2:ModifyVpcAttribute"


  ],
  "Resource": "*"
 }
 ]
}
```

VPC with Private and Public Subnet

Our second configuration for the VPC wizard will create a VPC having a private and public subnet, and it will provide us with a mechanism on how to launch a NAT instance or a NAT gateway. Consider the policy given below, which will allow the user to create either a NAT gateway or a NAT instance:

```json
{
  "Version": "2016-04-17",
    "Statement": [
     {
       "Effect": "Allow",
       "Action": [
```

```
                "ec2:CreateVpc",                "ec2:CreateSubnet",
"ec2:DescribeAvailabilityZones",
"ec2:DescribeVpcEndpointServices",

                "ec2:CreateRouteTable",         "ec2:CreateRoute",
"ec2:CreateInternetGateway",
"ec2:CreateNatGateway",

                "ec2:AttachInternetGateway",
"ec2:AssociateRouteTable",
"ec2:ModifyVpcAttribute", "ec2:DescribeKeyPairs",

                "ec2:DescribeImages",           "ec2:RunInstances",
"ec2:AllocateAddress", "ec2:AssociateAddress",

                "ec2:DescribeAddresses",
"ec2:DescribeInstances",
"ec2:ModifyInstanceAttribute",
"ec2:DescribeRouteTables",

                "ec2:DescribeVpnGateways",
"ec2:DescribeVpcs",             "ec2:DescribeSubnets",
"ec2:DescribeNatGateways"

        ],
        "Resource": "*"
    }
  ]
}
```

The policy shows how users can be allowed to launch instances
by use of ami-14f5cg3 only. Here is the policy:

```json
{
  "Version": "2016-04-17",
  "Statement": [{
    "Effect": "Allow",
    "Action": [

      "ec2:CreateVpc",                  "ec2:CreateSubnet",
"ec2:DescribeAvailabilityZones",
"ec2:DescribeVpcEndpointServices",

      "ec2:CreateRouteTable",          "ec2:CreateRoute",
"ec2:CreateInternetGateway",

      "ec2:AttachInternetGateway",
"ec2:AssociateRouteTable",
"ec2:ModifyVpcAttribute",

      "ec2:DescribeKeyPairs",     "ec2:DescribeImages",
"ec2:AllocateAddress", "ec2:AssociateAddress",

      "ec2:DescribeInstances",
"ec2:ModifyInstanceAttribute",
"ec2:DescribeRouteTables",

      "ec2:DescribeVpnGateways", "ec2:DescribeVpcs"
    ],
    "Resource": "*"
  },
                                {
    "Effect": "Allow",
    "Action": "ec2:RunInstances",
    "Resource": [
```

```
      "arn:aws:ec2:REGION::image/ami-14f5cg3",
      "arn:aws:ec2:REGION:ACCOUNT:instance/*",
      "arn:aws:ec2:REGION:ACCOUNT:subnet/*",
      "arn:aws:ec2:REGION:ACCOUNT:network-interface/*",
      "arn:aws:ec2:REGION:ACCOUNT:volume/*",
      "arn:aws:ec2:REGION:ACCOUNT:key-pair/*",
      "arn:aws:ec2:REGION:ACCOUNT:security-group/*"
    ]
  }
 ]
}
```

A VPC having Hardware VPN Access and Private and Public Subnets

The VPN connection will be created between the VPC and the Internet. The policy is as shown below:

```
{
  "Version": "2016-04-17",
  "Statement": [{
    "Effect": "Allow",
    "Action": [
      "ec2:CreateVpc",                    "ec2:CreateSubnet",
    "ec2:DescribeAvailabilityZones",
    "ec2:DescribeVpcEndpointServices",

      "ec2:CreateRouteTable",          "ec2:CreateRoute",
    "ec2:CreateInternetGateway",
      "ec2:AttachInternetGateway",
    "ec2:AssociateRouteTable",
    "ec2:ModifyVpcAttribute",

      "ec2:CreateCustomerGateway",
    "ec2:CreateVpnGateway", "ec2:AttachVpnGateway",

      "ec2:EnableVgwRoutePropagation",
    "ec2:CreateVpnConnection",
    "ec2:DescribeVpnGateways",
```

```
    "ec2:DescribeCustomerGateways",
"ec2:DescribeVpnConnections",
"ec2:DescribeRouteTables",

    "ec2:DescribeNetworkAcls",
"ec2:DescribeInternetGateways", "ec2:DescribeVpcs"

  ],
  "Resource": "*"
 }
 ]
}
```

VPC with Hardware VPN Access and Private Subnet Only

This will create only a private subnet and a hardware VPN access between the VPC and the network. Unlike in the previous options, in this option, we are not expected to have permission for attaching an Internet gateway to our VPC, and there will be no need for us to have permission for creating a route table and associating it with the subnet. It will be impossible for you to control the specific resources which can be used by a user. Here is the policy:

```
{
 "Version": "2016-04-17",
 "Statement": [{
```

```json
      "Effect": "Allow",
      "Action": [

        "ec2:CreateVpc",                      "ec2:CreateSubnet",
"ec2:DescribeAvailabilityZones",
"ec2:DescribeVpcEndpointServices",

        "ec2:ModifyVpcAttribute",
"ec2:CreateCustomerGateway",
"ec2:CreateVpnGateway",

        "ec2:AttachVpnGateway",
"ec2:EnableVgwRoutePropagation",
"ec2:CreateVpnConnection",

        "ec2:DescribeVpnGateways",
"ec2:DescribeCustomerGateways",
"ec2:DescribeVpnConnections",

        "ec2:DescribeRouteTables",
"ec2:DescribeNetworkAcls",
"ec2:DescribeInternetGateways", "ec2:DescribeVpcs"

      ],
      "Resource": "*"
    }
  ]
}
```

Management of a VPC

Creation or deletion of a VPC can be done from the page "Your VPCs." For you to view the VPCs as a user, you have to use the action "ec2:DescribeVPCs."

The example given below is for allowing the users to create and view VPCs on the page "Your VPCs," and then delete the VPCs which have been created with our first option of the VPC wizard, that is, the VPC having a single public subnet.

 The VPC has only one subnet which has been associated with the custom route table, and an Internet gateway which has been attached to it. For the user to be able to use the console to delete the VPC together with its components, they have to be granted permission to use a number of the "ec2:Describe*" actions, and this will enable the console to be in a position to check whether there exists some resources which are depending on the VPC.

Users must also be granted permission for dissociating the route table from our subnet, and then detach the Internet gateway from the VPC, and then add permission for allowing the users to delete both resources. Here is the policy:

```
{
  "Version": "2016-04-17",
  "Statement": [{
```

```json
      "Effect": "Allow",
      "Action": [

          "ec2:DescribeVpcs",   "ec2:DescribeRouteTables",
"ec2:DescribeVpnGateways",
"ec2:DescribeInternetGateways",

          "ec2:DescribeSubnets",
"ec2:DescribeDhcpOptions",
"ec2:DescribeInstances",
"ec2:DescribeVpcAttribute",

          "ec2:DescribeNetworkAcls",
"ec2:DescribeNetworkInterfaces",
"ec2:DescribeAddresses",

          "ec2:DescribeVpcPeeringConnections",
"ec2:DescribeSecurityGroups",

          "ec2:CreateVpc",                        "ec2:DeleteVpc",
"ec2:DetachInternetGateway",
"ec2:DeleteInternetGateway",

          "ec2:DisassociateRouteTable",
"ec2:DeleteSubnet", "ec2:DeleteRouteTable"

      ],
      "Resource": "*"
    }
  ]
}
```

Consider the following policy which will allow the users to delete only the Internet gateways and routing tables having the tag "Purpose=Test." It is impossible for users to delete individual route tables or the Internet gateways which do not have the tag, and similarly, the users will not be able to use the VPC console for the purpose of deleting a VPC which is associated with a different Internet gateway or route table. Here is the policy:

```
{
  "Version": "2016-04-17",
  "Statement": [{
    "Effect": "Allow",
    "Action": [


      "ec2:DescribeVpcs", "ec2:DescribeRouteTables",
"ec2:DescribeVpnGateways",
"ec2:DescribeInternetGateways",

      "ec2:DescribeSubnets",
"ec2:DescribeDhcpOptions",
"ec2:DescribeInstances",
"ec2:DescribeVpcAttribute",

      "ec2:DescribeNetworkAcls",
"ec2:DescribeNetworkInterfaces",
"ec2:DescribeAddresses",

      "ec2:DescribeVpcPeeringConnections",
"ec2:DescribeSecurityGroups",
```

```json
      "ec2:CreateVpc",                    "ec2:DeleteVpc",
"ec2:DetachInternetGateway",

      "ec2:DisassociateRouteTable",
"ec2:DeleteSubnet"

    ],
    "Resource": "*"
  },
  {
    "Effect": "Allow",
    "Action":  "ec2:DeleteInternetGateway",
    "Resource":
"arn:aws:ec2:REGION:ACCOUNT:internet-
gateway/*",

        "Condition": {
      "StringEquals": {
        "ec2:ResourceTag/Purpose": "Test"
      }
    }
  },
  {
    "Effect": "Allow",
    "Action": "ec2:DeleteRouteTable",
    "Resource":
"arn:aws:ec2:REGION:ACCOUNT:route-table/*",

        "Condition": {
      "StringEquals": {
```

```json
          "ec2:ResourceTag/Purpose": "Test"
      }
    }
  }
  ]
}
```

Consider the policy given below, which will allow the users to create and view security groups, and then perform addition and removal of inbound and outbound rules to any of the security groups which are associated with "vpc-14f5cg3." Here is the policy:

```json
{
  "Version": "2016-04-17",
  "Statement": [{
    "Effect": "Allow",
    "Action": [
      "ec2:DescribeSecurityGroups",
"ec2:DescribeVpcs", "ec2:CreateSecurityGroup"
    ],
    "Resource": "*"
  },
  {
   "Effect": "Allow",
   "Action": [
```

```json
        "ec2:DeleteSecurityGroup",
"ec2:AuthorizeSecurityGroupIngress",
"ec2:AuthorizeSecurityGroupEgress",

        "ec2:RevokeSecurityGroupIngress",
"ec2:RevokeSecurityGroupEgress"

      ],
      "Resource": "arn:aws:ec2:*:*:security-group/*",
      "Condition":{
        "ArnEquals": {
          "ec2:Vpc": "arn:aws:ec2:*:*:vpc/vpc-14f5cg3"
        }
      }
    }
  ]
}
```

Conclusion

We have come to the end of this guide. My hope is that you have learned how to use the AWS VPC. The Amazon VPC (Virtual Private Cloud) makes it possible for us to launch the resources of Amazon Web Services (AWS) into a virtual network which we have defined. The virtual network is the same as the traditional network which you would have operated in your own data center with the advantages associated with the use of the AWS scalable infrastructure.

Made in the USA
San Bernardino, CA
23 January 2017